*Occultism, Semi-Occultism
and Pseudo Occultism*

By Annie Besant

Copyright © 2021 Lamp of Trismegistus. All rights reserved. No part of this publication may be reproduced or transmitted in any form or by any means, electronic or mechanical, including photocopying, recording, or by any information storage and retrieval system, without permission in writing from Lamp of Trismegistus. Reviewers may quote brief passages.

ISBN: 978-1-63118-577-9

Esoteric Classics

Other Books in this Series and Related Titles

Aurora of the Philosophers by Paracelsus (978-1-63118-507-6)

Clairvoyance and Psychic Abilities by A Besant &c (978-1-63118-403-1)

The Feminine Occult by various authors (978-1-63118-711-7)

Rosicrucian Rules, Secret Signs, Codes and Symbols by various (978-1-63118-488-8)

An Outline of Theosophy by C W Leadbeater (978-1-63118-452-9)

Paracelsus, the Four Elements and Their Spirits by M P Hall (978-1-63118-400-0)

Essays on Ancient Magic by Helena P Blavatsky (978-1-63118-535-9)

Essays on the Esoteric Tradition of Karma by A Besant &c (978-1-63118-426-0)

The Use of Evil by Annie Besant (978-1-63118-532-8)

The Alchemical Catechism of Paracelsus by Paracelsus (978-1-63118-513-7)

Alchemy in the Nineteenth Century by Helena P Blavatsky (978-1-63118-446-8)

Qabbalistic Teachings and the Tree of Life by M P Hall (978-1-63118-482-6)

The Historic, Mythic and Mystic Christ by Annie Besant (978–1–63118–533–5)

The Hidden Mysteries of Christianity by Annie Besant (978–1–63118–534–2)

History, Analysis and Secret Tradition of the Tarot by Hall &c (978-1-63118-445-1)

Crystal Vision Through Crystal Gazing by Frater Achad (978-1-63118-455-0)

The Golden Verses of Pythagoras: Five Translations (978-1-63118-479-6)

Arcane Formulas or Mental Alchemy by W W Atkinson (978-1-63118-459-8)

The Machinery of the Mind by Dion Fortune (978-1-63118-451-2)

The A E Waite Reader: A Selection of Occult Essays (978-1-63118-515-1)

The Leadbeater Reader: A Selection of Occult Essays (978-1-63118-483-3)

Audio versions are also available on Audible, Amazon and Apple

Other Books in this Series and Related Titles

The Fourth-Gospel and Synoptical Problem by G R S Mead (978–1–63118–576–2)

On the Bhagavad-Gita by T Subba Row &c (978–1–63118–575–5)

What Theosophy Does for Us by C W Leadbeater (978–1–63118–574–8)

Spiritual Life for Man by Annie Besant (978–1–63118–573–1)

The Mysteries by Annie Besant (978–1–63118–572–4)

Fundamental Ideas of Theosophy by Bhagwan Das (978–1–63118–571–7)

Dreams: What They Are and Caused by C W Leadbeater (978–1–63118–570–0)

Communication Between Different Worlds by Annie Besant (978–1–63118–569–4)

Animism, Magic and the Omnipotence of Thought by S Freud (978–1–63118–568–7)

Buddhism by F Otto Schrader (978–1–63118–567–0)

Death by W W Westcott (978–1–63118–566–3)

The Religion of Theosophy by Bhagwan Das (978–1–63118–565–6)

The Spirit of Zoroastrianism by Henry S Olcott (978–1–63118–564–9)

The Brotherhood of Religions by Annie Besant (978–1–63118–563–2)

Fourth Book of Maccabees by Josephus (978-1-63118-562-5)

The Story of Ahikar by Ahiqar (978-1-63118-561-8)

Vision of the Spirit by C. Jinarajadasa (978-1-63118-560-1)

Occult Arts by William Q. Judge (978-1-63118-559-5)

Kali the Mother by Sister Nivedita (978-1-63118-558-8)

Love and Death by Sri Aurobindo (978–1–63118–557–1)

Interesting Account of Several Remarkable Visions (978-1-63118-553-3)

Audio versions are also available on Audible, Amazon and Apple

Table of Contents

Introduction...7

Occultism, Semi-Occultism and Pseudo Occultism...9

Occultism...31

INTRODUCTION

The word "esoteric" can be difficult to define. Esotericism in general can be seen less as a system of beliefs and more as a category, which encompasses numerous, different systems of beliefs. It's a bit of juxtaposition, since the word "esoteric" indicates something that few people know about, while the term itself broadly covers numerous philosophies, practices, areas of study and belief systems.

In a greater sense, Esotericism acts as a storehouse for secret knowledge, which is often considered ancient (by *tradition, if not by fact),* passed down from generation to generation, in private. At various times in history, simply possessing the knowledge of some of these subjects, was considered illegal and a jailable offence, if discovered. This usually included such general topics as Alchemy, Pharmacology, Qabalah, Hermeticism, Occultism, Ceremonial Magic, Astrology, Divination, Rosicrucianism and so on. Collectively, these areas of study were often referred to as the esoteric sciences.

Sometimes, the outer garment of a subject isn't esoteric, while what is hidden beneath it, is. As an example, Freemasonry isn't necessarily esoteric by nature *(*at *least not anymore),* but certain signs, passwords and handshakes given to the candidate during their initiation, are in fact, esoteric, in the sense that they are hidden from the general public.

Today, in the twenty-first century, such topics are readily available at bookstores across the country, and numerous mainsteam publishers offer beginners guides and coffee-table volumes on many of these subjects, intended for mass appeal. Books like *"The Secret"* have turned previously arcane topics into household knowledge. All that being the case, however, it isn't to say that there still aren't buried secrets to uncover, ancient wisdom being ignored and forgotten mysteries to be explored. In fact, it is often that we are only able to further our own studies by standing on the shoulders of these disappearing giants.

Lamp of Trismegistus is doing its part to help preserve humanity's esoteric history by making some of these classics available to those students who are seeking to unearth the knowledge of these ancient colossi.

So, be sure to check other titles from our *Esoteric Classics* series, as well as our *Occult Fiction, Theosophical Classics, Foundations of Freemasonry Series, Supernatural Fiction, Paranormal Research Series, Studies in Buddhism* and our *Christian Apocrypha Series*. You can also download the audio versions of most of these titles from Amazon, Apple or Audible, for learning on the go.

OCCULTISM, SEMI-OCCULTISM AND PSEUDO OCCULTISM

Speaking to the Lodge for the first time after returning from India, it will not seem to you, I think, either strange or inappropriate that I should take for my subject one which is largely drawn from Indian history; not the history of the outside nation, but the history of that inner line of thought which is of the deepest interest to us as students and as Theosophists. And inasmuch as history continually repeats itself, such a study may offer points of instruction to us in our own time. For I am going to ask you to consider with me what I may perhaps define - although definition is a little difficult - as, first, occultism, then what may be called semi-occultism, and, thirdly, the outgrowths which follow and surround these and which are specially marked and active at any time when true occultism is working in the world.

It is a very common blunder made by many people, to suppose that spiritual forces have in them something which they are pleased to call unpractical, and we continually notice an assumption, which is taken for granted without argument, that if a nation, for instance, should turn itself towards a spiritual ideal, or if individuals should devote themselves to the spiritual life, that then such a nation is likely to be undistinguished along other more evident and visible walks in life, and such an individual is likely to lose much of what is called his practical value in the world. Such a view of life is a blunder, and a blunder of the most complete kind. The liberation of spiritual forces, the setting free of energies on the spiritual plane, has a far greater effect both on the individual than can be produced by any of the forces that are started on the lower planes of life. When a spiritual energy is set free, it works down through the other planes of being, giving rise on each plane to a liberation of energy, and bringing about results great in proportion to the nature of the spiritual force. So that it is true in history, as you may find by study, that where spiritual forces are liberated, the intellectual life of the nation will also leap forward with tremendous energy, the emotional life of the nation will show fresh development, and even on the lowest plane of all - the physical, results will be brought about entirely beyond anything that could have been achieved by the energies of the physical plane which are set to work and which apparently cause these results. That is a principle, a law, which I will ask you to bear in mind through all that I have to say to you - that every force initiated on the higher planes, as it passes down to the lower, brings about results proportionate to itself; so that it is the shortest-sighted view of human life and of human activity which imagines that devotion to the spiritual life, the evolution of the individual in the spiritual world, is anything but an immense addition to all the forces of progress that work on the earth, anything but a lifting up of the world on the great ladder up which it is climbing.

But there is another principle that we must also bear in mind in our study, and it is this; that as forces are liberated on any plane, the results brought about by those forces will vary in their character according to those who utilize the energies after their liberation. As we have often pointed out to you here, energies on the different planes of nature are not what we call good or bad in themselves. Force is a force: energy is an energy. When we bring in the idea of good and evil, of right and wrong, of morality and immorality, these ideas are connected with the results brought about by individuals in the utilization of the forces. A time, then, of great spiritual energy, of great liberation of forces from the spiritual plane, will be marked to a great extent by activities of opposed characters on the lower planes of being, and those energies which are liberated on each plane may be taken up and used by individuals for what we should call either good or evil. The great mark of good or evil, looking at it from this standpoint, is the use that the individual is making of these forces, or such part of them as he is able to control; whether he is using them for the uplifting of humanity, whether he is regarding them as the Divine energy which he may use to forward the Divine purposes, or whether he is simply trying to grasp them for his own separate ends, striving to apply them to that which he desires to grasp and to hold, serving his own purposes without regard to the Divine economy. This, then, as I said, we will bear in mind in following out, first, as a lesson, something of the past in India, and then in applying the lesson that thus we learn to the movement which we know amongst ourselves at the present day, that great spiritual movement which is manifesting itself in the world and of which the Theosophical Society is one of the potent expressions.

To begin with, what is occultism? The word is used and misused in the most extraordinary ways. H.P. Blavatsky once defined it as the study of mind in nature, meaning by the word mind, in that connection, the study of the Universal Mind, the Divine Mind, the study of the workings of God in the Universe, the study therefore of all the energies which, coming forth from the spiritual center, work themselves out in the worlds around us. It is the study of the life side of the Universe, the side from which everything proceeds and from which everything is molded, the looking through the illusory form to the reality which animates it; it is the study which underlies all phenomena; it is the ceasing to be wholly blinded by these appearances in which we so continually move and by which we are so continually deluded; it is the piercing through the veil of maya and perceiving the reality, the one Self, the one Life, the one Force, that which is in everything and all things in it. So that, really, occultism, in the true sense of the word, may be said to be identical with that vision which, as you know, is spoken of in the Bhagavad-Gita, where Sri Krishna declares that "He who sees Me," that is, who sees the One Self, "in everything and everything in Me, verily he seeth." Such a study, if you understand at all what is implied in it, must necessarily mean the development in the one who sees of the highest spiritual faculties, for only by the Spirit can the Spirit be known. We speak continually of proving this, that, or the other spiritual thing. There is no real proof possible of Spirit, save through Spirit; there is no proof of the intellect, no proof of the emotion, no proof of the senses, which is proof when you come to deal with the reality of the Spirit. Nothing of the nature of proof along those lines, whether sensuous, emotional, or intellectual, can be anything more than a suggestion, a reflection of the truth, an analogy which may lead us on the right path, but proof in the true sense of the word it never can be. And it has been written truly in one of the great Indian scriptures, and repeated over and over again in the other scriptures of the world, that there is in the full sense of the word no proof of God save the belief in the Spirit, for only the Spirit that is akin to Him, and that is Himself, is able to know, is able to touch.

Now looking at real occultism as thus defined, realizing that no one can be in the full sense of the word an occultist save one in whom the spiritual nature is developed and active, we should, in our next step, be able to separate off from this true occultism very much that goes by its name both in the past and the present, amongst those who went before us and amongst ourselves today. But we should need, in separating off all these forms of so-called occultism, to distinguish between those which may be said, in a sense, to be stepping stones to the real, which were intended as steppingstones by those who gave them to the world and which may be used as steppingstones and utilized for progress, and other forms which are not really included under the name of occultism in any true sense of the term, those things which H.P. Blavatsky once spoke of as occult arts and which for many people seem to include everything they regard as occultism - arts in which certain forces of nature are utilized and in which faculties are developed on various planes in nature below the spiritual; for there are worlds above what we call the physical, but still below the spiritual regions, with which the development of certain faculties brings man into touch, enabling him to control and utilize their forces. There are almost a myriad arts and lines of study of this kind which ought never by any real student, by anyone who is seeking the higher truth, to be included in his thought when that thought is turned towards occultism. And some of you might clear up much confused thinking on this subject if you would refer to the writing of H.P. Blavatsky on *Occultism versus the Occult Arts,* where she draws the dividing line extremely clearly and shows the position that these occult arts hold, and should be recognized as holding, when we are dealing with human evolution.

True occultism, then, is that to which at first I would ask you to turn your thoughts, and its pursuit implies, as I have said, the development of the spiritual nature. Now the moment we speak of the development of the spiritual nature we must at once recognize that for the larger number of us that development must necessarily lie in the future, but that we may begin to work towards it today; that it is of enormous import to our true progress that we should recognize it and work towards it, and not, by misunderstanding the nature of that development, waste our time, waste possibly many lives, by following blind alleys and mistaken roads. The development of the spiritual nature must succeed - and this is one of the most important points that we can realize - must succeed the purification of the lower parts of our nature. We must be pure emotionally and intellectually, we must have reached a certain stage, at least, of the elimination of the personality before anything that can rightly be called spiritual progress is within our reach. No amount of mere intellectual development - and I will come back to that point, for I do not wish in any way to depreciate that most necessary line of human growth - but no amount of mere intellectual development will of itself bring about the growth of the spiritual nature. With the fundamental reason for that I shall deal more fully in a future lecture, but I must say in passing that the development of the spiritual nature and of the intellectual nature are on one vital point in direct opposition. The principle that we call the intellect is the analyzing, the dividing, the separative principle. The very purpose of its evolution is the building up of the individual, its root lies in the ahankara, or the "I"-making faculty, it is that which limits, which defines, which separates, which marks off the man from every other man, which makes what we may call that coating of selfishness which is absolutely necessary as one stage in evolution, which is one part of our growth in this world. It is a stage through which all humanity must pass, but which, regarded by itself, makes all those illusions which the Spirit transcends, and gives the touch of apparent reality to the separated self, the antagonistic self, the self that covets and grasps and holds and sets itself against all others. So that what we might call the very principle of illusion is represented by this intellectual faculty.

Necessary as its evolution is, none the less it is on this point in antagonism to spiritual evolution; for spiritual evolution means the recognition and the growth of the One Self into manifested activity, first within that sheath which has been formed by the intellect, and then by transcending it and bringing about that realized unity which is the object of our human evolution. It is for this that we place the unity of mankind in the spiritual regions, it is for this that we proclaim the brotherhood of man as a spiritual reality; for the Spirit is one, and it is only as that unity is recognized, consciously known - not simply intellectually seen, but consciously realized - it is only as that is done that the spiritual nature is in course of evolution. Inasmuch as the intellect is separative and the Spirit unifying, inasmuch as the one gives rise to illusion while the other transcends it, as the one is the source both of individuality and of personality, whereas the other is the source of that Oneship which we seek and shall realize - you will readily see how in the course of evolution these two parts of the nature cannot be regarded as causally related in the strict sense of the term, and we cannot say that by the evolution of the intellectual nature the spiritual nature will inevitably develop. On the contrary, we have to learn that we are not the intellect, but are to use the intellect as an instrument; that we are not the separated self, but the One Self living in all. That is the object of our evolution, that the goal of our pilgrimage; and therefore occultism, which means the study and the development of the spiritual nature, must transcend completely the intellectual evolution. It may even in many of its earlier stages find, and does find, its bitterest antagonist, its most dangerous enemy, in that very maker of illusions that you may remember we are warned against in *The Voice of the Silence,* that most spiritual book which so many of us have found as opening up the path to us to the spiritual life. Recognizing this, we shall naturally look forward to the spiritual evolution as a thing to be worked for rather than to be accomplished, from the stage at which we are at present. We should also be prepared to realize the immense difficulty of such an achievement, to understand how much will have to be done with the character and with the nature, how tremendous are the demands that we shall have to meet, before anything which in the strict sense of the term can be called occultism will be at all within our reach.

In the history of the past, where true occultism was the life of the world, where that great fount of spiritual life flowed from the Beings in whom the spiritual nature was wholly developed, when the world was drawing its light and its life from such Beings, it was obviously not possible that their knowledge, their powers, their work could be largely shared by undeveloped humanity, or even by the comparatively advanced humanity that surrounded them. Still less was it possible that any great part of their teaching or any true comprehension of their work and their methods could be known to the people at large; and yet it was necessary that links should be made, that steps, as it were, should be created. The result of this necessity was that men who were advanced - although in them the spiritual nature was not yet wholly evolved - men of great powers, who stand out in history as giants of humanity, strove to make possible for the advancing ranks of mankind some understanding of the upward path that should be trodden, some realization of the methods that might be adopted whereby approach might be made to the spiritual regions.

These men, great as they were, were not, as I have said, men in whom the spiritual nature was wholly developed, supreme, complete. Their evolution in many cases - and I speak with all reverence of those so much greater than ourselves - may even be said to have gone along one line in excess of other lines of their growth; so that one man might have enormously developed intellectual power but less perfection perhaps of moral character; another might have made great advance in devotion and might not have developed so much of intellectual force; another might be keenly alive to the religious necessities of man and not so much interested in his philosophical evolution; another, again, might have turned his attention towards the development of certain sides of man's nature which would touch the physical regions of existence, and even to the forcing of faculties in man, which, when built up from below, would bring him into touch with parts of the astral or the lower mental world, and might force those faculties and the part of his nature to which they belong in advance alike of mental and moral evolution. Along these various lines you will readily see that individuals might have progressed, and that each man would be characterized in his thinking and in his endeavor to serve mankind, by his own qualities, the attributes which he had specially evolved. So that, looking back into the ancient history of India, we find great teachers, Rishis as they were called, of many different types, each giving to the nation some great gift from his thought or from his knowledge, intended to help the more advanced souls of that nation towards progress which should end in spiritual evolution. Hence, to take one line of growth, the great philosophical system which we find in Indian thought, such a system, for instance, as the Vedanta. Regarded as an intellectual system of pure philosophy it puts in a magnificent intellectual form a view of the Universe, of the One Self, of the One Life, and of its manifestations, as illusory in the deepest philosophical sense, that serves as an intellectual training, as a step which men must take in learning something of the mysteries of the Universe. This system, when studied apart from the Yoga that alone can make it practical, may be classed under the head of semi-occultism. It is a system true within its own realm, a system intended to help forward the progress of mankind, only capable of being grasped, of being followed, of being studied, by souls already advanced in mentality; but none the less it is not the spiritual truth; it is only an intellectual presentment of one aspect of it, an intellectual showing forth of one side of it.

It is a thing that must always be remembered, that the Spirit can never be expressed in terms of the intellect, that the One can never be grasped in the terms of the many, and that any intellectual presentment of spiritual truths must necessarily be partial, must necessarily be imperfect, must be, as has often been said, a colored glass through which the white light is seen; a ray is passed through the prism of the intellect which breaks up the white light of the Spirit, showing it in varied colors as these scattered beams, each one of which is imperfect in itself. One, then, of the great gifts to ancient India coming in this way as the result of true occultism, as the result of the mighty spiritual life, was the philosophy of the Vedanta and all those intellectual systems intended for the training of man, and giving, so far as the intellect could give it, a view of the spiritual reality. But remember the saving clause, "as far as the intellect could give it". The intellectual view is only a partial view; and such a view, however much it may help man to see intellectually something of the possibilities of the higher life, can never make him realize it in consciousness, or give the true knowledge which comes alone through the evolution of the spiritual nature itself.

Along another line of activity would come the many schools of Yoga. These schools, as you well know, were exceedingly various in their nature. Some of them were designed to develop the higher intellectual consciousness in man by means of concentration, by means of meditation, and thus to bring him into touch with the higher regions of his being; they were intended to lead him, stage by stage, to get free from the body, to pass consciously into higher worlds, so that his consciousness might function in those more extended realms of being. And we find many of the teachings of Yoga - you may read many of these systems at your leisure, those which come under the great classification Raja Yoga - carefully adapted to aid the growth of the mind, the evolution of the loftier mental faculties, the rising on to the higher intellectual planes, the passing into states of consciousness far beyond the reach of ordinary humanity. They are again, a steppingstone offered, but still coming under this heading that I have called semi-occultism. Other schools were founded which dealt with man in different fashion, which strove to force his faculties from below, to force the evolution and the training of the astral faculties, to bring him first into touch with the astral world, to make him familiar with a part of the phenomenal universe closely allied to the material. These have generally been classed as the schools of Hatha Yoga, and in them various methods were employed dealing with the lower vehicles of man. By these methods the body was trained, was to a great extent purified and rendered an obedient instrument. The power of the will was also enormously developed, the man was taught to be master of his lower nature and so to take what in very many cases was a real step upwards, although we cannot include it in any sense of the term under the heading of true occultism.

It must be remembered when dealing with all these schools, when looking at them and striving to learn alike their use and their abuse, that it is a great thing for a man to become master of his passions, it is a great thing to subject the animal nature, to be able to stand unshaken, no matter what temptations may assail the lower man. And very, very many of these schools, which it is often the fashion in the West to scoff at and despise, have yet in them this element, that they at least recognize that man's intellectual nature should be master of his sensuous nature and that he should learn complete control over the body, complete control over the passions. And even along many of the darker lines of evolution, even in the schools that tread the path which all those who would reach the highest should most carefully avoid, it is none the less true that the subjugation of the lower nature is most rigorously insisted upon. It is only the ignorant who suppose that those darker schools are all given over to sensuous practices. Many of the followers of those schools lead lives which, so far as that side of the nature is concerned, might be taken as examples by an enormous majority of the men of the western world.

Now the whole of these different schools rose and flourished in ancient India as the result of the great down pouring from the spiritual regions on to the lower planes, and naturally they were used both for selfish and for unselfish purposes. But in dealing with all those schools of Yoga which train the intellect and develop the high forms of intellectual consciousness, it is well to remember that they are real stepping stones to the higher, and that it is a necessary stage of our progress that we should practice concentration, that we should use meditation, that we should be accustomed to contemplate intellectually and emotionally the ideals which appeal to us by their grandeur and their nobility. Those are stages in our upward path, and stages that very many of us might well be utilizing now, with a view to the higher growth, the deeper wisdom of the future. Men took up these varying lines of evolution, stirred fundamentally by the prompting of the Divine Life within them, ever seeking to raise them and to help their upward growth; stirred, so far as they themselves were conscious, by the natural and rightful desire for higher evolution, for further progress, for growth in life. For, as we have often seen when we have been studying progress, we cannot leap at a bound to the heights of the spiritual life; we have to climb step by step, we have to utilize the higher thoughts in us for the subjugation of the lower, and then in turn to outgrow that higher when a greater height comes within our sight and without our reach. We have learnt, as we know well, in our studies, that we may constantly eliminate lower ambitions by nourishing a higher ambition, and that, though that higher ambition be still attached to the personality, or even transcending the personality, be attached still to the individual, it is none the less a steppingstone, it is one of the ways by which we climb. It is well continually to kill out our lower by our higher desires, though even those higher in their turn seem lower as we are rising above them and greater perfection comes slowly within our gaze. So that this longing for a higher life, this desire to develop, this yearning for progress, had, and have, their rightful place in evolution; and it is out of the ranks of those who feel these, out of the ranks of those who use the methods which make progress possible, that are taken those who are capable of further evolution. They learn gradually to transcend the hope for individual progress, and learn that that also, in the fullest sense of the term, is illusion and cannot exist as life which is spent as part of the Divine Life, pouring itself out for others; and no life is true, no life real, no life spiritual, save when the very idea of the separated life is entirely transcended, and all the thought of the being, all the energies of the life, are poured forth as part of the One Self and no distinction is recognized. Service is then the natural expression of the life, helping is that in which the true existence is felt. But ere it is possible that this ideal can be even intellectually realized, some progress, at least, must have been made in transcending what we recognize as the personality; and it was in order to make that possible to every man immersed in illusion, as all men have been and are, that the various methods were suggested by those who would fain help their fellows forward, as steps on the upward path.

Others, seeing in the religious instinct in man - in that side of his nature allied to the emotions, in which devotion finds its root and the possibilities of its growth - seeing in that his easiest upward path, gave to the world the various forms of religion in all their variety of adaptation to human needs, thus making the path upwards suitable for those whose constitution attracted them chiefly in the direction of love and of service. Seeing, then, that all these methods of growth were most active at the time when the real life was working at the heart of things, it will not be difficult to understand how, as that life found fewer channels for its expression in the world, fewer who were ready to transcend their own limitations and to give themselves wholly as channels of the Divine Life, all these methods lost their vitality and a great part of their usefulness. And so we find, in looking around the India of today, that many of those things that were living are now dead, that many of the systems that were vital are now mere shells, forming subjects for intellectual controversy or for individual pride, but no longer stepping stones to the higher life. Here and there, still some gleam of the true life survives, some real use is being made of these stepping stones upward; but so far as the great masses of the people are concerned, mere shells and forms remain - evidences of what existed in the past, evidences, may we dare to hope, of what may be in the future.

It is hardly worth while to remind you that while semi-occultism may serve as a steppingstone to real occultism, pseudo-occultism is generally a distinct obstacle and hindrance. Under this heading may be classed as the "occult arts", in the study of which many promising beginners have lost their way and wasted their lives. Geomancy, palmistry, the use of the tarot, etc., all these things are well enough for those who want to tread the byways of nature and to gather knowledge of her obscurer workings. They may be harmless, interesting, even useful in a small way, but they are not occultism and their professors are not occultists. A little success in their pursuit - and success does not demand high qualities of either head or heart - is apt to breed the most absurd vanity and pretentiousness, as though this dalliance with the apsaras of the kingdom of occultism converted a commonplace man into one of its rulers, a mage. A man may be past-master of all these arts, and yet be further away from occultism than is a pure and selfless woman seeking only to love and to serve, or a generous, clean-souled man, devoted to helping his fellows. And if these arts be turned to selfish purposes, or if they nourish vanity, their professor may find himself approaching perilously near to the gateway of the left-hand path.

Looking for the application of this to our present movement, the lesson springs easily enough to our gaze. Again, in our own days, a great outpouring of real life has occurred, again an effort has been made by those who are the guardians, the Reservoirs, of that life for our humanity, to pour out the true spiritual energies for the helping and the uplifting of man in every region of his being, the manifesting again of the possibility of the real life. This has been marked by certain definite statements made from time to time, by hints thrown out here and there by her who was the special messenger in our own day of this possibility opening up for our own race. And there is one passage in that paper to which I referred at the beginning, which gives us in a phrase the reality of life: we are told that when a man becomes a real occultist he becomes only a force for good in the world. Here is a sentence that people read without realizing at all its meaning, a sentence that comes in the middle of many other statements, and does not strike with its full force on the unprepared mind and heart. For many things may be said which are missed for want of receptivity, and many truths are proclaimed which remain dark and silent, save to those whose eyes are beginning to be opened to see, and whose ears are beginning to be opened to hear. And that statement, which really puts the occult life in a few words, is one that most readers pass by without realizing its significance. There is no true spiritual life, there is no real occultism, until the man at least recognizes that the goal of his living is to become a force for good, and that only, in the world. He is no longer to seek his own progress, no longer to seek his own life, no longer to seek his own development - no longer to ask aught that heaven or earth or any of the other worlds can give him for himself. There is only one thing left within him, the longing to be of service: only one thing the motive of his being, to be a channel for the great life of God, to enable that life to be scattered more effectively over the world of man, and over all worlds where that life exists.

When that is recognized, even afar off, when that ideal first dimly dawns upon the human heart - come it by way of intellectual apprehension of its sublimity, or by way of devotional recognition of its truth - then for the first time the spiritual life stirs within the man, the first germ of the spiritual nature begins to quicken into life. And so we begin to realize that if true occultism would be reached and understood by any of us, we should have to begin the preparation for it by working at character in the way that every religion has taught. How often do we hear it said amongst ourselves:

> "*We know all these moral truths, there is nothing new in Theosophy when it simply reiterates the old morality. When we are told to be unselfish, to seek to help others forward, to eliminate the personality, to kill out our faults, it is all an old story that we have heard to weariness. We want something new, we want some fresh knowledge, some facts of the astral world, some strange things of the mental region - that is what we demand from Theosophy, that is what we are seeking, and we do not desire to have pressed upon us these ethical maxims, these continual repetitions, these old-world stories which every religion has made familiar, and which we can hear from any pulpit.*"

And yet the truth of the matter is that along that path only the spiritual life has been and is possible for man; that the Divine Teachers who gave the religions to the world with their perpetual insistence on morality, gave them knowing the spiritual life, and knowing that only along that line the real progress of man into unity with God was possible. And when it was again declared by the lips of the Christ that only he might gain his life who lost it, that those who would be perfect must sacrifice all that they had, when he again reiterated the ancient teaching that narrow was the path and straight was the gateway, he was only repeating what all true occultists have taught as to the necessity of the training for the spiritual life.

As progress is made, all those methods of Yoga which tend to help forward the individual, which are followed in order to gain progress, practiced in order to evolve faculties, and used in order that the individual may faster forward himself - all these are dropped, and Yoga is regarded, not as the means of self-evolution, as we are accustomed to regard it here, but as the using of great forces for the lifting and the helping of humanity, with utter disregard for the going forward of him who is using them, with no thought of progress on the part of him who is wielding them for the helping of man. For in truth all control of higher forces, all utilization of these vast energies, ought to come only within the grasp of man when he has transcended the personality and has learnt to use them only for the helping of all. We readily admit this in the common things of life, and recognize the difference between learning the use of an instrument and mere holding an instrument without knowing how to use it. A pen, for example is one of the most useful of instruments, but its utility depends upon the brain and the heart behind it, upon the knowledge and the skill that wield it; and a pen in the hands of a child is of no more use than any fragment of wood that the same child might pick up to use as a toy in its play. Very much the same is the grasping of the forces of the superphysical world by those who have not yet conquered the lower nature, eliminated personal desires and consecrated themselves wholly to the divine service. They are, truly, picking up an instrument which may be used for the highest and noblest ends; they are, truly, placing their hands upon a tool, which in hands that know how to use it, may serve for the salvation of the race; but unless the spiritual nature be developed, that tool fails in its highest purposes, that instrument fails in all its noblest possibilities. And it has this peculiarity, that whereas the pen that I used as a symbol might be comparatively harmless in the hands of the child, the grasping of those forces by one in whom the personality is not eliminated may become a source of danger alike to himself and others, and may tend to retard the progress of the race instead of lifting it upwards. That is why some of us who have learnt but the mere alphabet of these great truths, lay so much stress - stress to weariness, as I know some of you think when I am speaking to you - on the moral training which must precede all attempt at occult study. H.P. Blavatsky gave us the same lesson when she herself said that she had blundered in teaching part of the alphabet of occult knowledge without insisting upon that old precept that the moral growth must come before the occult training, and that the character must be purified, raised and spiritualized before anyone should dare to lay his hand upon the latch of the occult gateway. Hence it is that those qualifications that we have so often studied are made qualifications for initiation; hence it is that there has even been the demand that only the pure should enter, that only the selfless should come in.

If I have spoken of the past to you tonight, if I have reminded you that amongst us today the very outburst of the new spiritual life will cause activity on all the lower planes, it is because I would bring the experience of the past to reinforce a lesson so often given from this platform, it is because I would warn you of the dangers that surround us on every side - dangers that some of us are beginning keenly to recognize, and to recognize just because they have to some extent struck us, and have therefore made progress the more difficult. So that it is our duty as Theosophists, as would be students of the science of the soul, to be careful that in all things character precedes any attempt at the gaining of power, that purity, selflessness, devotion, utter self surrender, be found in us ere we touch the Ark of occultism - for without these any success is a defeat, without these any attempt is doomed to failure. And surely it is better for us to learn from the experience of the past than by the bitter suffering that grows out of the personal experience of today; better to learn by the authority of the Great Teachers who have proclaimed the lesson over and over again, than to have to learn it by the suffering that follows from grasping powers ere we are ready to use them, from plucking the fruit of knowledge ere it is ripe for our consumption, from striving to rule ere yet we have learnt to obey, and from endeavoring to snatch at the mighty forces of the spiritual realm until we have learnt that great lesson of the Spirit - that only by giving is the Spirit shown, that only by utter abnegation is the true life realized. As the very life of God in manifestation is a life that gives everything and asks nothing back, so those who would reach unity with Him and realize what the spiritual life means, must learn to give and not to take, to help and not to hold, to pour out without seeking or looking for return. Only as we learn that, do we become fit candidates for the higher knowledge, only as the heart is thus rendered absolutely pure may we dare to face the presence of the Master, hoping that when "He looks at that heart He may find no stain therein."

OCCULTISM

H. P. Blavatsky defined Occultism as "the study of the Divine Mind in Nature," and it would be difficult to find a nobler definition. All life, all energies, are hidden, and only their effects are patent. The forces by which a jewel is crystallized in the womb of the earth, by which a plant develops from a seed, by which an animal is evolved from a germ, by which a man feels and thinks — all these are occult, hidden from the eyes of men, to be studied by scientists only in the phenomena of growth, of evolution, as these present themselves, while the impelling forces, the nature of *vitality*, the invisible, intangible, secret springs of all activities, these remain ever hidden.

Moreover, this admirable definition posits Mind behind all the manifestations which we totalize as *Nature*. It is these manifestations which are woven into that garment by which we see God ("and weave for God the garment thou see'st Him by"). His Mind is revealed in natural phenomena, and by the visible, "the invisible things . . . are clearly seen". Bruno spoke of natural objects as the divine language; they are the Self-expressions of God. In the divine Mind exist the Ideas which are to be embodied in a future universe; the world of mind, the *Intelligible World* precedes the material world. So taught the Hebrews; so taught the Greeks; and the teaching is confirmed by our everyday experience. We think, before we embody our thought in an action. Ere a man creates a great picture, he must have the idea of the picture in his mind; he *thinks it out* before he paints it on the canvas. It is the world of Ideas, the Intelligible World, which is the realm explored by the Occultist.

He seeks to understand this hidden world whence flow all outer manifestations; to grasp the Ideas which embody themselves in varied forms; to seek the hidden sources of life and to trace their outflow, as the physical scientist seeks and traces physical types and their evolution. He is the scientist of the invisible, as the ordinary scientist is the scientist of the visible, and his methods are scientific; he observes, he experiments, he verities, he compares, and he is continually enlarging the boundaries of the known.

The Occultist and the Mystic differ in their methods as well as in their object. The Occultist seeks knowledge of God; the Mystic seeks union with God. The Occultist uses Intellect; the Mystic Emotion. The Occultist watches Ideas embodying themselves in phenomena; the Mystic unfolds the Divine within him that it may expand into the Divinity whose Body is a universe. These sharp-cut definitions are, of course, true only of abstract types; the concrete individuals shade off into each other, and the perfected Occultist finally includes the Mystic, the perfected Mystic finally includes the Occultist. But on the way to perfection, the Occultist must evolve, *pari passu,* his consciousness and the successive vehicles in which that consciousness works; while the Mystic sinks into the depths of his consciousness, and cares naught for the bodies, which he disregards and abandons. To borrow two well-known terms: the Occultist tends to become the Jīvanmukta, the liberated Spirit residing in material bodies; the Mystic tends to become the Nirmāṇakāyas, the liberated Bodiless One. The Occultists rise, grade by grade, through the Hierarchy;

the Mystics become the Nirmānakāyas, the Reservoir of Spirituality, from which are drawn the streams which irrigate the worlds. Blessed, holy and necessary are both types, the two Hands of the One LOGOS in His helping of His universe.

Bearing in mind H. P. Blavatsky's definition, we can readily see how the more ordinary view of Occultism, that it merely means the study of the hidden — without defining the hidden — inevitably grows up. The Occultist is to study the Divine *Mind in Nature* then he must not only expand his consciousness, so as to enter into the Divine Mind, but must also evolve his subtle bodies and their senses, in order to contact Nature in all the grades of subtlety of her manifestations. This evolution of the subtle senses and the knowledge gained through them of the phenomena of the subtle, or superphysical, worlds of matter — loom large in the eyes of the superficial observer, and he comes to identify Occultism with clairvoyance, clairaudience, traveling in the subtle bodies, and the like. It would be as sensible if this same good gentleman identified physical science with its apparatus — its microscopes, telescopes, spectroscopes. The subtle senses are merely the apparatus of the Occultist, they are not Occultism. They are the instruments by which he observes the objects which escape the normal physical eye. As the ordinary instruments of science may have flaws in them, and so may distort the physical objects observed, so may the super-physical instruments have flaws in them, and distort the superphysical objects observed. Mal-observation with a defective instrument does not vitiate the scientific method, though it may for the moment vitiate particular scientific conclusions. The same is true as regards mal-observations with ill-evolved superphysical senses; the occult method is scientific and sound, but for the moment the particular conclusions drawn by the Occultist are erroneous. Where then is safety? In repeated observations by many observers — just as in physical science.

Let us examine this a little more closely. A scientific observer finds his observations through his microscope yield him a certain picture; he draws what he sees. Then he puts a higher power on his microscope, and again observes the object; he obtains another picture. He compares the two. He finds that certain parts of the object that he thought were isolated from each other are connected with threads so fine that they were invisible under the lower power. His first observations were accurate, but incomplete. One result of such incompleteness is that every scientific man, in giving pictures of objects as seen through the microscope, notes on them the power of the lens through which he observed them. Again, if a young observer, on comparing his drawings with those made by experts and inserted in the textbooks, finds that he has inserted something not seen in the others, he will test his lens and repeat his observation, taking another object, identical with the first, lest some dust, or hair, or other accidental intruder should have presented itself unbidden for his inspection. Let us apply this to the student of Occultism. He has evolved a power of sight beyond the normal; he observes some etheric object, and puts down his observations; a few years later, having evolved a higher power of sight, he observes the object again, and finds that the two parts of it he thought successive are divided by some intermediate process. I will take an exact instance. Mr. Leadbeater and myself in 1895 observed that the ultimate physical atom, being disintegrated, broke up into the coarsest form of astral matter. In 1908, observing the same process again, with a higher power of sight evolved during the intervening years, we saw that the physical atom, on disintegration, ran through a series of further disintegrations, and re-integrated finally into the coarsest form of astral matter. The parallel with the lower and higher powers of the microscope is complete.

Once more; a young observer sees some astral form; he compares it, if he is wise — he is not always wise — with previous observations of older observers, or with statements by great seers in world-scriptures. He finds his observation unlike theirs. If he is a serious student he tries again, making repeated and careful observations, and finds out his mistake. If he is foolish, he proclaims his mal-observation as a new discovery.

But, it may be said, people respect the physical scientist, and accept his observations, while they mock at those of the Occultist. All the discoveries of new facts were mocked at before the public was ready for them; was not Bruno burned and Galileo imprisoned for declaring that the earth moved round the sun? Was not Galvani called *the frogs dancing-master* when he laid his finger on the hidden force now called by his name? What matters the mockery of ignorant men to those whose steadfast eyes are seeking to pierce through the veils in which Nature shrouds her secrets?

So far as the methods of observation of the material side of Nature are concerned, observations carried on by means of improved apparatus — externally manufactured or internally evolved — the methods of physical and of superphysical science are identical. Knowledge is gained by study of the results obtained by predecessors in the same field, and by observations directed to similar phenomena, with a view to verifying or correcting the results.

The evolution of the consciousness which observes through the senses is another matter, and this plays a greater part in occult than in physical science; for consciousness must unfold as higher senses evolve, else would the better tools be useless in the hands of the inefficient workman. But the object of physical and superphysical science alike is the extension of the boundaries of knowledge.

Is this extension desirable or not? If the knowledge be turned to human service, yes; if to the increase of human misery, no. The application of physical science to the destruction of human life is most evil; yet not for that can we seek to block the advance of chemistry. The Occultist who knows how to liberate the forces imprisoned in the atom will not place within the hands of the competing nations of the world this means of wholesale destruction. Yet he knows that chemistry is advancing in this direction, and that it must not be hindered in its advance.

As regards the Occultists themselves they are useful or dangerous according to their motives. If they are devoted to the welfare of the worlds, then their rapid evolution is beneficial. If they seek power for their own aggrandizement, then they are dangerous. The evolution of consciousness is all to the good, for, as that unfolds, the wider view brings the man gradually more and more into unison with the Divine Will in evolution, and, at a certain point in this expansion, he inevitably recognizes the all-compelling claims of the larger Self. But in the lower stages, in the astral and mental worlds, while his self-discipline must be rigid as regards his bodies, pride and selfishness may make him a danger to his fellow men. The discipline of the senses and the control of the mind are equally necessary, whether the man is aiming at development for service or for individual aggrandizement. He must lead a life of rigid temperance in all things, and he must become master of his thoughts. But if personal ambition rule him, if he seek to gain in order that he may hold, not in order that he may give, then every added power becomes a menace to the world, and he enters the ranks of the Adversary. The Occultist must evolve into a Christ or into a Satan — to borrow the Christian terms. For him there is no half-way house. Safer are the green pastures where the flock may feed at peace than the arid heights, with their crevasses and their precipices, with their shrouding mists and their crashing avalanches. None who has trodden part of the rugged way would seek to induce others to enter on it. But there are some whom an imperious inner force compels; some who cannot rest by the still waters, but must seek to climb the heights. For such the way is open, and for them there is no other way which is possible. Only, that they may not add their shattered lives to the "wrecks which strew the path of Occultism", let them gird their loins with strength, let them don the armor of purity and the helmet of unselfishness, and then let them go forward, in the Name of the World's Redeemers, with their eyes fixed on the Star which shines above them, careless of the stones which gash their bleeding feet.

www.ingramcontent.com/pod-product-compliance
Lightning Source LLC
LaVergne TN
LVHW041503070426
835507LV00009B/781